Yate & District Labour History Group

The Miners' Strike

1984-85

ISBN: 978-1-291-98208-4

Copyright © Colin Burgess 2014

All rights reserved, including the right to reproduce this book, or portions thereof in any form. No part of this text may be reproduced, transmitted, downloaded, decompiled, reverse engineered, or stored, in any form or introduced into any information storage and retrieval system, in any form or by any means, whether electronic or mechanical without the express written permission of the author.

Colin Burgess,
Thornbury
May 2014

Photo by John Harris: Photo reproduced by permission of The People's History Museum. Also see
Sean Matgamna (2014) Class Against Class: the miners` strike 1984-85, London, Phoenix Press.
For more photos of the Police/Army in action see Mark Metcalf, Martin Jenkinson, & Mark Harvey (2014) Images of the Past: The Miners` Strike, Barnsley, Pen & Sword Books Ltd.

Acknowledgements

We are grateful to the Yate & District Heritage Centre for the initial stimulus to discuss the issue of the political nature of materials stored in their archives, and the published work forming part of the research material for the booklet. In particular we were pleased with the work on the slave trade in Bristol and South Gloucestershire. This pointed the way ahead when it came to writing up our research.

People who have contributed to the research have been Mike McGrath, Brian and Ann Fletcher, and my son, researcher and project manager Clive Burgess without whose aid nothing would have been created, to all of whom I offer my thanks. Similarly my thanks and commiserations go to all the people who have tackled different versions, reading in the hope of finding enlightenment perhaps, only to be puzzled by the unfamiliar language: but this new language or rather, way of understanding, is exactly the point of the exercise. Beyond this are the people who have understood and encouraged me "not to give up writing": peace and socialism, sisters and brothers!

The same message goes to John Harris, whose photographs of the miners` strike still convey the atmosphere of the time, and whose picture of the police in action he gave us permission to use on our front cover, see Sean Matgamna (2014).

Without my grandson, Steffen Burgess, whose technical expertise was an ever ready help with the mysteries of the computer, and without whose knowledge I could not have coped when I was hacked by the alienated wild cards, I could not have completed this study. I cannot forget Mike and John, the printers, who have bound the many copies I have submitted to them. . . even to extent of investing in a new system of binding the A4 sheets to make an excellent workmanlike booklet. Many thanks. And finally to Bob Hall who taught me how to use the P.C. some years ago, and still finds the formula "State monopoly-capitalism with a liberal-democratic ideology" to be a mind-stopping experience.

Abstract

This brief essay was written in the 30th anniversary year of the last great miners` strike. It opens with a quote from Ian Lavery MP launching the Orgreave Truth and Justice Campaign, and his Early Day Motion in Parliament calling for the investigation of police activities during the 1984-85 miners` strike. The essay reaches back to Rafael Samuel`s (1986) oral history published as *The Enemy Within: pit villages and the miners` strike of 1984-84,* referring to Prime Minister Thatcher`s labelling of the miners at the time.

The methodology used in the essay was a model mapping the social reality of class, from which the structure of the essay was derived. The development of the essay analysed the similarities and differences between slavery and free labour in the Bristol and South Gloucestershire area, and the right to withdraw activities from production whilst negotiating wages and working conditions. Much of the materials used for this section of the essay is grounded in work published by Yate and District Heritage Centre on the history of the mining industry in the area. Using our model of class, the first three aspects of class at which we looked, namely the social structure changing from feudalism to capitalism, the conflicting interests of the owners and the producers, and their practices of everyday life, tend to be objective. These aspects of social reality focus on the structural bottom line from which consciousness and activity spring. The second three, community, consciousness and struggle, on the contrary, tend to belong more to the top line of the model, the engagement of subjectivity in activities, and the resulting experiences.

The second section of the essay looks at the ideological struggle carried on in the local newspaper by some of the residents of South Gloucestershire. The Yate and Sodbury Labour Party takes centre stage in this section. The background to the letters was the continuing attempts by government to re-organise British economic structure and life. There were reports throughout the year of long-running strikes throughout the economy. In the primary sector, of course, was the year-long strike in the nationalised extractive industry, the miners. In the secondary sector, manufacturing was represented by a strike at British Aerospace, and in the tertiary sector the teachers' strike continued on. The opposite sides of the miners' strike were taken by Miss Olive Seller a hard–right supporter of Mrs Thatcher, and Roy Middleton, a long-time socialist and remedial teacher. A Liberal-Democrat and a seasoned Tory emerged locked in struggle, but nothing shifted the focus on the police activities and the miners' responses. In the ideological struggle as reported by the newspaper the explanation was reversed into the miners' activities and the police's response.

The final section is devoted to a discussion of the government's production and use of Nicholas Ridley's Report of the Nationalised Industry Policy Group, a sub-committee of the Conservative Party's Economic Reconstruction Group. This became the plan for the whole strategy of privatisation; the key concept is "fragmentation" – of nationalised industries and, possibly by chance, of "the working class". What was then called "Thatcherism" came to be what is now called "neo-liberalism", part of the liberal-democratic ideology which masks state monopoly-capitalism.

Contents

Preface

Section 1. Introduction

Section 2. Methodology

2a. Theory

Diagram: mapping the social reality of class

2b. Method

    i.   Research areas

    ii.   Research topics   iii. Research materials

Section 3. Development: working class history and biography

3a. Our model and the relationship between labour and slavery in historical South Gloucestershire

3b. The use of our theoretical model in research

    i.   Class structure   iv. Class community

    ii.   Class consciousness   v.   Class interests

    iii.   Class practices   vi. Class struggle

Section 4. Empirical work: Readers' letters – the miners' strike and the police

4a. Ideological struggle in the community.

4b. Discussion of Gazette readers' letters

Section 5. Class struggle: the miners' strike in historical perspective

5a. The ruling class and the miners

5b. Contemporary class struggle

5c. Privatisation and the boundary between state monopoly-capitalism and liberal-democratic ideology

Section 6. Conclusions.

Reading list, Newspapers,

Index.

Preface

This essay started out as a discussion of labour history and the local Heritage Centre between Mike McGrath, Brian and Ann Fletcher, and myself Colin Burgess, in Mike`s front room. It is this group of people, members of Thornbury and Yate Constituency Labour Party, who formed the nucleus of Yate and District Labour History Group. Their concern was on access to the local Heritage Centre for labour history material. At that meeting Colin said that he would produce a labour history pamphlet suitable for inclusion in the Centre`s Open Day Fair. The present booklet began as notes towards the writing of such a pamphlet, but the topic selected seemed important enough and interesting enough to become further involved, in especially in a thirtieth anniversary year. So the notes and their possible pamphlet became a booklet which may or may not seem to the Centre to be as "value-free" as that of the liberal-democratic people writing their books on the technology and ownership of the mining firms of Yate and district.

The whole issue exposed the nature of the British ruling class and its establishment of the US liberal-democratic way of life in Britain during the second major breakdown of capitalism in the twentieth century. The extension of the Kondratiev long wave theory of economic activity relates our experience of the last 100 years: the depression of the years from 1925 to 1950, the affluence of 1950 to 1975; and the new depression of 1975 to 2000 should according to this theory have been followed by a period of affluence from 2000 to 2025. However, despite the stimulus provided by the US/UK arms industries and the new colonial wars of the new millennium, this has not proved to be the case. The slump of 1975 and the failure of the Labour Party to produce a unified left-wing alternative, provided the Conservatives the excuse to export whole manufacturing industries abroad and to replace them with "service" industries, specifically finance and banking. The resulting focus on money produced a credit boom, resulting in the collapse of trust throughout the financial system and a national debt allowing the government to declare that a long period of "austerity" was needed to recover our financial health. The liberal-democratic way of life, in the mean-time finally allowed the political Right to dismantle collective provision for health, education, welfare and travel in collaboration with transnational corporations.

The miners` strike has to be understood against this background. John Bloxam et al in (2014) *"Class Against Class: the miners` strike 1984-85"* wrote,

> "The ruling class had spent years planning and preparing this class war. They were united behind the Tory government. They were using the state power against the miners with little restraint or inhibition. That government waged a coordinated and long planned class war on the three decisive fronts of the struggle: in industry, in the politics that was so central an aspect of the strike, and in the crucial propaganda war against the miners."

Our booklet focuses on the history of the industry, the political use of the police to force a resolution to the strike, and the ideological struggle carried on in a local newspaper. It is a book to be studied as part of that ongoing struggle.

Colin Burgess
Thornbury
May 2014

The Miners' Strike 1984-85

Section 1. Introduction: The problem and our orientation

In November 2012 Labour MPs were circulating an early day motion (EDM), demanding an investigation of the policing of the 1984-85 miners' strike. The EDM originated from the launch of the Orgreave Truth and Justice Campaign. It was tabled by Ian Lavery, Member of Parliament and former National Union of Mineworkers' president. He is quoted by the Morning Star (Wednesday, November 28th 2012) as saying, "I believe there should be an enquiry into the whole of the police's activity during the strike. Miners were accused of crimes they did not carry out. They were frightened out of their wits." Some of the historical evidence for this now almost forgotten event in labour history is contained in the oral history research published in *The Enemy Within: pit villages and the miners' strike of 1984-5* by Routledge & Kegan Paul in 1986, edited by Raphael Samuel et al. It was published as the journal of the History Workshop series. The dedication is to the "Durham Mechanics, the most ancient of the mining trade unions (c.f. W.S. Hall, *A Historical Survey of the Durham Colliery Mechanics Association 1879-1929*) and now leaders of the 'Justice for Miners' campaign." (Orgreave JusticeCD £9-99, http://bit.ly/1AYchbR)

As a topic relating Yate & District to the wider course of labour history we believe that 1984-5 local response to the policing of the strike is worth spending some time investigating. In his preface to the oral history, Rafael Samuel wrote:

> "When we started work on this book, in February 1985, convening a 'History Workshop' on the strike, and inviting miners and their families to a working weekend at Ruskin College, Oxford, we argued – in the words of the invitation – that the meaning of the strike would not be determined by the terms of the settlement – if there is a settlement – or even by

the events of the past year but by the way in which it is assimilated in popular memory, by. . . retrospective understanding both in the pit villages themselves and in the country at large".

So, in our search for the retrospective understanding of this critical moment in labour history, one of our key witnesses is the souls of the miners and their families bound in a journal of the History Workshop. The best biographical introduction to the miners' strike and the solidarity of their communities available now is Catherine Paton Black (2012) *At the Coal Face: my life as a miner's wife*, London, Headline Publishing Group (price £6-99p). Another dimension is provided by Jeremy Deller's exhibition of *English Magic* at the Bristol Museum and Art Gallery, Queen's Road, Bristol 12th April to 21st September 2014. Hal Foster in the booklet accompanying the exhibition writes, ". . . for Deller, as for latter-day Gramscians such as Ernesto Laclau and Chantal Mouffe, democracy is also *dissensus."* Foster continues,

> "Deller presents in a painted mural, a `futuristic vision of a popular insurrection` [which] shows St Helier, the capital of Jersey and notorious site of offshore banking, put to flames in a 2017 riot over taxes. . . This leads us to a related notion also crucial to Deller, *civil war*, which is explicit in his signature work of the last decade, *The Battle of Orgreave* (2001), a mass restaging of a violent confrontation between police and miners during a 1984 strike (some 200 miners from the original conflict participated in the filmed performance, along with 800 veterans of historical re-enactments)."

We start from a piece of concept clarification in relation to records of historical research in the Yate & District Heritage Centre on the one hand, and on the other, some empirical investigation of the contemporary understanding shown by the people of the Northavon constituency, as demonstrated in the pages of the

Gazette 1984-5. We have provided a Reading List at the heart of the book, but also given details of references at the point of use.

We will take our task from Raphael Samuel (1986) as he outlined in the preface to the History Workshop publication.

> "The proper job of a historian, if intervening in a matter of public debate, is explanation, not adding to the chorus of recrimination and blame nor treating the actors as sovereign agents, but showing, or attempting to show, the ways in which history is made behind our backs, in spite of our best intentions rather than because of them. Where others see events, the historian looks for process, in which a thousand different circumstances conspire. Where others see high level decisions, the historian will look for the unspoken premises of any action, the hidden determinations which it obeys, [and] the unforeseen consequences which result from it. Where others offer images far clearer than any reality could be, the historian disrupts the narrative, and asks what is happening off-stage."

For Yate & District heritage, the most relevant chapter in Samuel's book is chapter 8, by Barbara Bloomfield on the Women's Support Group at Maerdy. This pit described itself as the last pit in the Rhondda, and was one with which Yate Labour Party identified and which it "adopted". This labour history group project aims to dig out some memories of the past, held by people still living, by written scraps of past time in minutes of meetings, contemporary newspapers, or organised rationally in books, in "histories" of this and that. The purpose is to complement the existing oral history published by the Yate and District Heritage Centre, the focus of which tends to be on geological and technological details and the local community, rather than labour history.

Because the notion of "working class" is not used much today, we have begun from the position of sociological history so that we can be clear about our notion of the social reality of "class". In the first place we are using a functional view of the major institutions of capitalist society: family, class and the state. Therefore the realities of our categories are the owners of capital, the producers of goods and services, and the controllers of the processes of production, distribution, exchange and consumption. In another place we have analysed the social reality of the Thatcherite project to replace production with financialisation. We are not using the notion of status: upper class, middle class and lower class, which depends on people's own definitions of the prestige of national social positions. Nor are we using market research categories like classes A, B, C1, C2, D and E referring to professional and administrative occupations, higher supervisory, lower supervisory and clerical positions, skilled manual, semi skilled manual and unskilled manual workers, or to up-dated versions of Mosaic. Finally, we are not using the Registrar General's social classes, which were used to sort out the 1801 – 1966 national census data. For an up-to-date discussion of the concept of 'class' see the journal of the British Sociological Association, Sociology vol. 48, no. 3, June 2014. Our producing class are the people on whose work our lives depend in the most direct way. At present we are looking at the coal mining industry because that is one focus of Yate & District Heritage Centre's publications on industry. We can do similar research on agriculture, the family historian's ubiquitous "Ag. Lab." and/or research on the factories of Yate and district. In fact we wish to make a start comparing the producing class as free wage-earners with those living as slaves, starting with Lorna Brooks and David Hardill (2008) *Anti-slavery in South Gloucestershire.* What we wish to do here, is to insist on our producers as 'labour', not as 'consumers', nor as the current fashion has it, as 'plebs', or citizens within slave city-states.

Section 2. Methodology:

2a) Theory

Our theoretical position attempts to examine the processes underlying the appearances reported by the participants in the events of the miners` strike, which preceded, maintained and flowed from the actions of the people involved.

The diagram below aims to map the aspects of social reality usually referred to when people are discussing the differential distribution of wealth, power and prestige among the families of a given society, for example, the concepts of class structure or class consciousness. The State has emerged over the last thousand years to stabilise both the territory and the possession and uses of wealth, power and prestige by families. During that time the nature of British society has shifted from tribal, through feudal to capitalist, and records of people`s biographies illustrate the evolution of these relationships.

On a shorter time span, see Catherine Paton Black (2012) for a focus on biography, and Goran Therborn `Class in the 21$^{st}$ Century` in *New Left Review 78 Nov/Dec 2012* for a post-modern historical view of class from the beginning of May Day in Chicago 1886 to the `loose, decentralised networks` of resistance to capitalism of 2011. Therborn`s analysis of class is continued as `New Masses? In *New Left Review 85 Jan/Feb 2014*.

It is important to remember Marx`s caution here. ""Society does not consist of individuals, but expresses the sum of inter-relations , the relations within which these individuals stand. As if someone were to say: seen from the perspective of society, there are no slaves and no citizens: both are human beings. Rather, they are that outside society. To be a slave, to be a citizen, are social characteristics, relations between human beings A and B. Human being A, as such, is not a slave. He is a slave in and through society," (Grundrisse)

Mapping the social reality of class

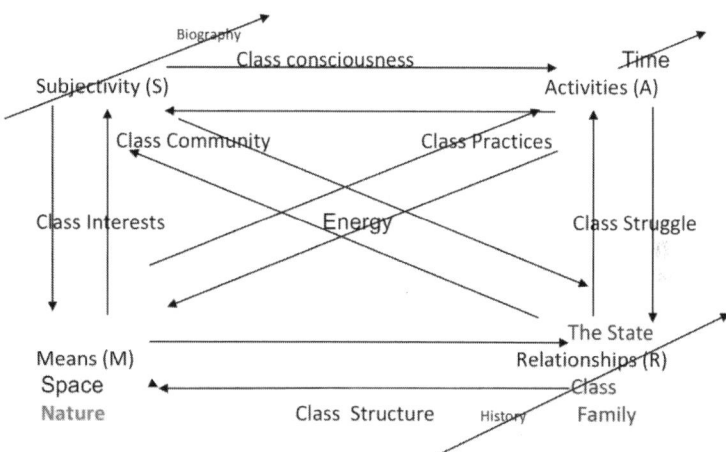

[Note: This diagram is the intellectual property of Colin Burgess, whose name should be quoted as its author. He can be contacted on crburgess@btinternet.com]

The diagram makes a frame of reference for the essential elements of these concepts and the inner relations between them and other concepts. The framework is capable of holding all concepts useful to the analysis of social reality; therefore it is necessary to include only those which are relevant to the work in hand. As in social reality itself, the elements, inner relations and emergent aspects do not cease to exist by becoming invisible. They are always lurking in the background. Class interests, for example, are rarely mentioned by New Labour politicians who prefer to use the lower middle class notion of class values. However class interests can be seen in everyday life arising from the possession or lack of physical (dwellings, environment, transport), biological (health, medical care, food and clothing) and cultural (ownership, education, entertainment) means. So-called higher classes possess more of these means of subsistence, lower classes possess fewer of the means of subsistence. In less "developed" societies people generally live closer to nature.

2b) Method

Using class analysis in relation to our experience of labour in general, and Yate and district in particular, we hope to be able to research individual case studies of labour in South Gloucestershire. Starting from the published work of the Yate and District Heritage Centre, our aim is to unearth labour history in its own right through critical reading and empirical investigation. We have used six major historical sources, three emphasising the subjective side of human experience and three emphasising the objective side. Two are on the topic of Bristol and the slave trade, one oriented subjectively, the other oriented objectively. The other four are on the topic of the miners' strike of 1984-5, again one approaching it subjectively, the second oriented objectively, while the third book is again objective, and the fourth is oriented subjectively.

So, on the slave trade we have Peter Fryer (1984) *Staying Power: the history of Black people in Britain*, Atlantic Highlands, Humanities Press Inc. and Robin Blackburn (1988) *The Overthrow of Colonial Slavery 1776 – 1848*, London, Verso. On the miners' strike, we have Rafael Samuel et al. (1986) ed. *The Enemy Within: pit villages* and *the miners' strike 1984-5*, and Huw Beynon (1985) ed. *Digging Deeper: issues in the miners' strike*, London, Verso, the third book, Seumas Milne (2004) *The Enemy Within: the secret war against the miners,* London, Verso, examines the strike again, objectively, after twenty years, and the fourth book Hywel Francis (2009) *History on Our Side*, Ferryside, Iconau, gives the story subjectively, what

Beatrix Campbell of the Guardien calls " [an] eloquent memoir of the strike".

Sean Matgama ed. (2014) *Class Against Class: the miners` strike 1984-85* with photos by John Harris, has a broader approach to the strike. It is available from http://www.workersliberty.org/history/strikes-and-trade-union-history/miners-strike-198485 Our theoretical model offers a way of reading these works in relation to each other, see also R.S.Neale (1985) pages 169-172

2c) Research Areas:

To see the inner relationships between the elements of social reality from which these aspects of the social reality of class emerge, see the diagram.

 i   Class Structure
 ii Class Interests
 iii Class Practices
 iv Class Community
 v   Class Consciousness
 vi Class Conflict

2d) Research Topics

i. Theory and the relationship between labour and slavery in South Glos
ii. Class struggle: Yate people, the 1984-85 miners` strike and the State.

2e) Research Materials

Benwell Community Project (1979) *Final Report* Series No. 6 *The Making of a Ruling Class*

Lorna Brooks & David Hardill (2008) *The History of Anti-Slavery in South Gloucestershire,* Yate & District Heritage Centre

Hywel Francis (2009) *History on Our Side*, Ferryside, Iconau
Seumas Milne (1994) The Enemy Within: the secret war against the miners, London, Verso

Steve Grudgings et al (2008) *Kingswood Coal*, South Glos. Mines Research Group (SGMRO)
Steve Grudgings (2009) *Frog Lane Colliery – sixty years on,* SGMRG and the Yate & District Heritage Centre

Nicholas Ridley (1977) *Final Report of the Economic Reconstruction Group*

Dexter Whitfield (1983) *Making it Public: evidence and action against Privatisation,* London, Pluto Press

Editions of *The Gazette* for 1984 and 1985 stored in Thornbury Library:
Editions of *The Morning Star* for 2009, available from morningstaronline.co.uk
William Rust House, 52 Beachy Road, London, E3 2NS

Section 3. Development: Working Class History and Biography – a critical re-interpretation: some first points of interest and connections:

3 a) Our model and the relationship between labour and slavery in South Gloucestershire

Eric Hobsbawm (1969) *Industry and Empire,* one of our historical authorities, writes in his introduction, "To write about this country without also saying something about the West Indies and India, about Argentina and Australia, is unreal. Nevertheless, since I am not here writing the history of the world economy or of its British imperial sector, my references to the outside world must be marginal." We are therefore delighted that Yate & District Heritage Centre has included in its publications *The History of Anti-Slavery in South Gloucestershire* written and edited by Lorna Brooks and David Hardill.

The function, (whatever the intention) of *The History of Anti-Slavery in South Glos. (HASG),* is to demonstrate the normality of slavery in British society. However, using class analysis and the stand-point of the labourers, we can take some points of interest and prise open the liberal-democratic ideology used to construct the text. For example, on page 26 of *HASG* we read:

> `Many local industries were linked with the slave trade: the brass works at Warmley produced "Guinea Goods", which were sold to the slave traders; sugar refiners and distillers were dependent on slave labour for their raw materials; whereas the miners in Kingswood produced the coal needed to fuel these various processes.`

From a functionalist viewpoint, this is correct. However, the implication seems to be that "they were all in it together", in other words, the labour force was mining coal to exploit their fellow-workers overseas. Perhaps the weight of interpretation falls on the awkward word "whereas". If we go back to the top of page 19 of *HASG*, the authors have a section on "The Beneficiaries" which throws more light on the situation. They write:

> "Many Bristolians profited from the trade, and the local area as a whole flourished during this time. The wealth obtained from the slave trade was used to fund new ships, buildings and factories. Bristol`s first bank, which opened in Broad Street in 1750, was founded by slave merchants. The bankers provided loans to finance new ventures in the trade. Indeed much of Bristol`s wealth came about as a result of the slave trade. Profits from the slave trade made many traders very wealthy men indeed, not least Edward Colston."

3b) Use of our theoretical model in research

The first three aspects of class, structure, interests and practice, tend to emphasise the objective aspects of social reality, and the second three tend to bring out the subjective aspects, community, consciousness and struggle. The first three may be studied quantitatively, the second three are more open to qualitative analysis. However, it is important to realise that these aspects are all reliant on the inner relations of the four elements of social reality: subjectivity, and the three more objective elements, activities, means and relationships; and that the resultant of the dialectical interaction of the four is what is referred to as "social reality". The totality can be seen through the diagram from which we are abstracting the aspects to examine them and then replacing them into the model.

i) Class structure

The changing class structure from feudalism to capitalism is well brought out in Steve Grudgings (2009), which we highlight in the following paragraph. Our diagram locates three institutional clusters of social relationships in its bottom right-hand corner: families, classes and the State. Our class structure has three major classes: the owners of capital, the controllers of expected activities appropriate to the social positions of the persons involved, and the producers of goods and services required by the population. Examples of the uneven development of ownership class relations are given in Steve Grudgings (2009). Grudgings writes that the shallow coal seams had been worked out by 1700 but that local holders of feudal landowning titles such as the Player family who held the manor of Frampton Cotterell, the Dennys family of the Serridge estate, and especially Samuel Astry, Lord of the manor of Westerleigh. Astry's three daughters "married well" and after Astry died in 1704, the Westerleigh property passed to Jarret Smith, Alexander Colston and Thomas Willoughby (Lord Middleton). Jarret Smith who had land at Mayshill which he was already mining, led the way in acquiring mineral rights for the land. The invention and use of the Newcomen steam pumping engine enabled miners to dry out the mines so that coal seams could be worked at much deeper levels. According to Grudgings, the Bragge family, which succeeded the Player family as Lords of the manor of Frampton Cotterell, installed the first engine in the district at Nibley in 1750, followed by Jarret Smith at Coalpit Heath in 1751 and again in 1763. The development of capitalist society over the next hundred years changed the nature of the owning class, and of the controllers who were separated out from the producers. The account of these years is given in much greater detail by Matt Southway (2008) in *Kingswood Coal*. Handel Cossham, a successful local entrepreneur, is quoted by Steve Grudgings (2009) as recording in his diary that in August 1855 he went underground "at Frog Lane in the High Vein with John Cook the Bailiff (the colliery agent or manager)". Cossham seems to have been interested to inspect the possibilities of the nearby Parkfield Colliery "in the same seams on land leased from the Lords of Westerleigh". The feudal titles of Lord and Bailiff are still used although Grudgings provides a more up-to-date interpretation in brackets. He continues:

> "During 1855 and 1856 The Coalpit Heath Colliery Company (CPHCC) appear to have commissioned a large body of survey work from Alex Bassett of Cardiff (Lord Tredgar`s Surveyor) and a number of these very finely drawn and coloured maps survive."

The surveyor and the colliery agent or manager as highly skilled and "responsible" workers, whose activities are performed in association more with the owners than the producers, were matched by supervisors and clerical workers who were more in touch with the producers than the owners. Steve Grudgings in describing people who had been colliery managers writes,

> "There would always have been one or more undermanagers (so-called because they work UNDER the overall manager and managed work UNDERground). The only name we have is Bob Sharpe who is fondly remembered by some of our interviewees. Unfortunately we do not have any pictures of any of these gentlemen."

The fluid nature of this new capitalist control class can be exemplified through Matt Southway`s (2008) brief biography of Handel Cossham. Cossham had been a colliery clerk who taught himself geology and mining engineering, and married his employer`s daughter. Following Southway`s timeline we see Cossham as an entrepreneur carrying out an "intensive survey" in 1851, which led to him successfully re-opening pits previously thought to be worked out. Then as director of the firm of Wethered, Cossham and Wethered he was developing separate collieries in Speedwell and Deep Pit from 1861, and again in 1867 Cossham and Wethered started up Kingswood Coal and Iron Company. He then bought the Lordship of the manor of St George, and its mineral rights, as well as the Lordship of the manor of Stapleton and its mining rights from the Duke of Beaufort. In 1879 he bought out the Wethered family and set up a limited company, attracting one of the sons of W.O. Wills the tobacco magnate as a shareholder. Other shareholders were senior members of Cossham's staff, so the man who had been a colliery clerk now had his own staff, demonstrating the social mobility typical in a society with an expanding social structure.

The functional position of the producers is different in kind from that of the owners, in that they are not able to live on inherited or acquired wealth without wages earned by working for others. The difference from controllers is that they also lack the necessary cultural capital and family circumstances, the qualifications which would make the work of commanding others seem congenial. In capitalism competition to enter the control class, to remain, and to make any progress in it, is physically and emotionally wearing and ever present. Not everyone wishes to follow in Handel Cossham's footprints. However, without the activities of the producers there really would be no wealth, no goods or services useful or marketable, produced. Even the machines increasingly used to take the place of labour are themselves the embodiment of past labour activity. Labour history is about these people.

Ii Class interests

'Interests' can be seen objectively by taking up issues that arise in the course of everyday life, and observing the class nature of the people involved. They are the long-term divisions of wealth, power and prestige necessary to maintain the lives of people in social reality. We can examine the class interests of the producers and the owners more clearly than we can the control class, because the producers' and the owners' interests are more clearly separated, whereas the top controllers' interests have more in common with owners' and the lower controllers' interests have more in common with the producers' interests. In this way, then, we can also see back from issues in everyday life through interests to the social reality of class structure.

If we take the coal producers, then we can look at what seem to us the most significant issues in their practices, as discussed by the oral history interviewees, reported by Steve Grudgings (2009) and Matt Southway (2008). These issues were, and still are, wages, skills, health and safety, family life and strikes. It is strikes that often bring workers into direct contact with the State. The most important of the coal producers were the "face workers". Working in physically demanding conditions, in the dark with only minimal lighting and primitive tools, they were the most highly paid workers. Grudgings writes "We don't have any face workers contributing to our Oral History, so our accounts of underground work are based on deductions and photographs." One of the Oral History interviewees, Fred Drew, then a young unmarried farrier, said that he got about two pounds something a week. At roughly the same time (1947) my uncle, a ganger on the Southern railway got about two pounds and fifteen shillings, and my father, as a plumber, got three pounds and ten shillings. Fred Drew continued, "the men didn't get much more, underground they'd get about a fiver or something, but for the job they did, they did it for that, well it was stupid. Then that's the way it was all those years ago, we're going back what, 'cor Lord what how many years?" These comments show the continuing understanding of producer class interests over the years.

Using class analysis it is possible to divide up the money received from the sale of what workers by hand and brain have produced into two parts: the necessary value and the surplus value. The `necessary` value is money from the sale of goods and services that are given as wages for workers to buy what is necessary to feed, clothe, house and warm, maintain in health, educate and entertain themselves and their families. This money must be enough for these workers to return fit to work on the following day, and for their children to grow into people fit and strong enough to carry on life into the future. The surplus value is what is left to the capitalist after that is paid. From this has to be deducted the rent paid to the landlord and the rest of the firm's overheads. It is this "surplus" that Abraham Darby accumulated and then invested in the Baptist Mills Brass Works. The necessary value of the producers' lives is given by Kathyrn Sherrington in Grudgings (2009) as "family life and the woman's role". She writes,

> "Standards of living for most Frog Lane miners were low and would remain so until well after 1949. Accommodation for mining families was often owned by the colliery company, while other homes belonged to the Lords of the Manor of Westerleigh. Floors were normally bare and very cold, while some families made mats from rags and old clothes, creating make-shift carpets to walk on. Stan Williams of Coalpit Heath was born in 1928 and remembers his mother's floor coverings; rags sewn together in beautiful patterns to make floor mats."

For free workers, the lower limit of necessary value is the maintenance of the worker's ability to return to work on the following day able to produce the same amount and quality of goods and services as they had done today. For slaves, their owner decides what constitutes his slaves' living wage, but the same principle is involved. The example of Leopold II, King of the Belgians, in his late nineteenth century Congo "heart of darkness" (that is, working "his" labourers to death) is not possible as the long term basis for capitalism. See Joseph Conrad in Adam Hochschild (2006) *King Leopold's Ghost*, London, Pan books, and use of slave labour for extracting sap from vines in the Congo for the new rubber industry. It is, however, the extraction of surplus value from the work of the labour force, slave or free, that is called "exploitation" in class analysis. If this is not possible the firm will be forced by circumstances to close down. The term comes from mainstream economics to refer to the use by business people of "the factors of production" namely land, labour and capital. It is in this sense that

Matt Southway (2008) writes in *Kingswood Coal* of Leonard, Boult and Co. as "a firm who exploited and developed many of the local collieries at different periods".

Iii Class practices

To be able to produce goods and services, all workers, free or enslaved, have to develop sufficient skills to use in their employers` service. Fred Drew`s description of re-sharpening the pick-axes used by the face workers shows exactly what is meant in this division of miners` labour. He says,

> "Repair the picks, you know the picks you drive in to get the coal out, you had to sharpen those most days unless you were lucky in that you didn`t break them off. It would depend on how you`d harden them; if you hardened them too much they`d drive in the stone and break the ends off and they`d be useless and then you`d have to temper them right as well and you`d harden them off, if you did it too hard then they`d break. So what you did, you put it in the fire, shaped the ends and then let him cool off. Then get the heat going, then put them back in and bring them out, dip them in the water quick and you`d rub the stone down, the pick down with the stone and watch the colours go down get to blue, in the water and that was it. We did it to save straw and dipping in the water guarantee to break the end off like with a chisel. We used to do chisels the same way, and temper them in the same way. If you did see blue in the straw [colours of the steel as it cooled], then it was OK, that was the right thing that tempered them then, the blue came and then you`d test them on the anvil. Get the hammer and chisel on the anvil and if it didn`t break off they knew it was all right. If it broke off you had to do it all over again. It was as simple as that."

All the producers' skilled work is as detailed as this, each in its own way, although not all is described in the Heritage documents available, and all producers' activities contribute to the final product as does the blacksmith's. One of the blacksmith's tasks, in which Fred Drew as a farrier would have been a specialist, was the shoeing of the pit ponies, and Steve Grudgings has useful descriptions and photographs of this work.

A new book on the background to the miners' strike gives a comment on the use of picks in mining. Bernadette Hyland reviewing Catherine Paton Black (2012) *At the Coal Face: my life as a miner's wife* for the Morning Star December 1012, writes,

> "[Catherine Paton Black] gives sharp insights into conditions in the pits, commenting that working conditions there during the 1940s and '50s were primitive." Black writes, "Before the modern machines arrived Doug's father and brothers were at times quite literally going at parts of it with a pick axe. They were all injured at some point."

An area of all work that has now been recognised as important is "health & safety". As production has become less individual and more co-operative, socially organised, and capital-intensive, international organisations have developed new norms such as "the duty of care." Part of this new outlook is the notion of "risk". Risk assessment can be seen as class-based. The capitalist risks his or her capital when investing it in an enterprise, it must always produce surplus value to be re-invested and it may disappear altogether if the firm fails. The controller risks his power/authority over the people whose activities he/she is charged with controlling – the aspect of control over activities and reproduction of relationships, always raises the possibility of resistance and the transformation of relationships. The producer, without capital or qualifications and a career, and selling "only" his/her skilled labour power especially in physically dangerous work like mining always risks his health and safety.

It may be useful here also to refer to the difference between labour on the one hand, and capital and land on the other. For class analysis, labour is the only creative factor of production. Capital is the accumulated value of past labour. Land is that part on nature which labour has made useful for human production. We start with Subjectivity (S), that is, the top left-hand element of our diagram above. In a famous statement of this, Karl Marx (1868) *Capital I* p. 157, wrote:

> "We presuppose labour in a form that stamps it as exclusively human. A spider conducts operations that resemble those of a weaver, and a bee puts to shame many an architect in the construction of her cells. But what distinguishes the worst architect from the best of bees is this, that the architect raises his structure in imagination before he erects it in reality. At the end of every labour-process, we get a result that already existed in the imagination of the labourer at its commencement. He [read `he or she`] not only effects a change of form in the material on which he works, but he also realises a purpose of his own that gives the law to his modus operandi, and to which he must subordinate his will. And this subordination is no mere momentary act. Besides the exertion of the bodily organs, the process demands that, during the whole operation the workman's will be steadily in consonance with his purpose. This means close attention. The less he is attracted by the nature of the work, and the mode in which it is carried on, and the less, therefore, he enjoys it as something which gives play to his bodily and mental powers, the more close his attention is forced to be."

Iv) Class Community

The work of both the slave and the free miner was carried on under these stringent subjective and objective conditions. "Labour is, in the first place," Marx wrote, "a process in which both man and Nature participate, and in which man of his own accord starts, regulates and controls the material reactions between himself and Nature." He goes on to say that in changing the world, men and women change themselves. The origins of class consciousness and community can be glimpsed through the eyes of people like miner Fred Woodruff and Phyllis Taylor, long-time member of the GMB and (Northavon) Labour Party. Discussing the dangerous conditions in which men worked underground in the mines at Frog Lane Colliery, Coalpit Heath, Mr. Woodruff said,

> "Everybody worked together and everybody helped one another and that was it. There was nobody being nasty against each other. Same as when you got under that ground, down that ground and underneath, the atmosphere seemed to change, everybody was for one another and everybody helped one another".

However, in many cases this atmosphere did carry over to the community above ground. In discussing community life in Winterbourne after the end of mining at Frog Lane, and many more people moved into the area, Phyllis Taylor spoke about missing the friendliness and support of the small villages where the miners and their families lived. Sarah Morris reports her as saying,

> "Everybody knew everybody else. It's not like it is today, I mean there are people here who I couldn't tell you their names and they never even speak. . . It's sad really, and it's not being nosey but everyone used to help one another."

The objective difference between free and slave labour is the difference of relationships. The most immediate difference is that free people always have the possibility of combining to withdraw their labour from use by their employers, in order to gain some concession, whereas enslaved people can do this only at grave risk to themselves. The withdrawal of free labour has come to be called "striking". However, whereas the obedient slave has provisions ensured, the unemployed or striking free worker receives no wages. The three more qualitative aspects of social reality are intertwined, especially so in the case of the mining communities, but they are separate aspects in their own right.

Returning to `Slavery and Brass`, we have one of the Coalbrookdale heroes of Arnold Toynbee`s "industrial revolution", Abraham Darby the first. The authors write:

> "Abraham Darby established the Baptist Mills Brass Works in 1702 with surplus money from his expanding slave trade business. William Champion founded his own brass works in Warmley in 1746. The brass works at Baptist Mills used 2,000 horse loads of coal a week; the coal came from coal mines in Kingswood, which had been operating since medieval times.
>
> The brass industry was so commercially important that factory keyholes had to be blocked-up to prevent competitors spying. The majority of brass workers did not know where the goods they were making ended up and indeed, in many ways, the workers were exploited themselves."

These phrases make it possible to shift from the functionalist perspective to our class perspective, whilst retaining the notion of classes that are functional for capitalist social reality. In shifting perspective we will continue to use aspects of our model of class in researching part of labour history in Yate and district. The biographies of people like Abraham Darby, Handel Cossham, Fred Drew and Phyllis Taylor are bound up with labour history and we shall continue to add more to what we have understood so far. The history of pits like Frog Lane colliery has provided the conditions of existence for the lives of working people in Yate and district, in the South Welsh valleys like the Rhondda, in Nottingham and Yorkshire. Labour history is about the inner relations of these aspects of the social reality of industrial life.

v) Class consciousness

Returning to Steve Grudgings' presentation of the Frog Lane Pit, we can extend our analysis further into working class history through the paragraph following Fred Woodruff's memories of working underground.

> "It was very much a 'macho' world too, this tone was set by the men working at the coal face where the hard and dangerous work made them the highest earners in the pit. For all these reasons it's no surprise that coal miners were therefore regarded with a little fear and awe even in their own communities. Coal miners were at the forefront of early workers' movements such as Chartism, Trade Unionism and Communism. "

Writing of what our perspective sees as the concentration of ownership, Matt Southway also has a brief mention of what he calls "twentieth century troubles". In 1899, Cossham's pits employed six hundred men who raised 77,000 tons from Deep Pit and 54,000 tons from Speedwell pit. Southway writes,

> "The colliery was purchased by a new company, The Bedminster, Eaton, Kingswood and Parkfield Collieries Ltd., who also owned the Hanham Colliery at that time. Their head office was at first at Easton Colliery, but after the closure of those pits in 1911 in a period of labor troubles, the management moved to Speedwell. Labour troubles continued

and the writer can well remember, as a boy, seeing the striking pitmen in procession down through Lawrence Hill with their candles in their caps. (The pits were mainly non-fiery). There was much local hardship, children going to school barefoot for lack of footwear and `feeding centres` being opened up in local drill halls etc., to provide a mid-day meal for the children whose fathers were on strike."

Class consciousness is always sharpened by the onset of group trouble. Catherine Black writes (page 95) that,

"The mining industry was never far from the headlines at that time. The Tories had used a slogan a few months earlier, in February 1974, which read: `Who governs Britain?` alongside a picture of some miners. Heath had called a snap election that had led to a hung parliament. There was real anger from the government about how powerful the miners` union had become. But in our eyes they were merely ordinary hard-working folk voicing an opinion. A proud hard-working class who kept the country running and the lights on. To be part of it would in many ways feel like an honour."

In terms of political class consciousness, however, there are clear stages in the development: from the idea of being "a citizen", one of the ordinary hard-working folk to a member of "a proud hard-working class" of which it is an honour to belong. This is completely compatible with being a member of a trade union, even a trade union on strike. The shift to the next stage is through recognising the limitations of this activity within the existing framework of capitalism. The next stage then is in joining the Labour Party and campaigning to change the laws of the country in order to protect and further the interests of the working class and thereby society as a whole. The fourth stage of class consciousness may never be reached, but logically is to understand the limits of parliamentary politics, and join a revolutionary socialist association, such as the Socialist Workers Party, or the Communist Party.

Catherine Black's situation can be seen as she moves from page 95 through page 182, where she explains, "We've never been 'political' people although we were life-long Labour voters. Government was only something we took notice of if I managed to catch the *News at Ten*, half asleep on the sofa, or if a particular strike affected our day-to-day lives, like the bread strike." Further politicisation never occurred, as can be seen on page 307, where at the end of a union demonstration in Norwich. "As we left that day, a man came up to me and took off a red star he was wearing on his lapel. I knew it had something to do with socialism but beyond that I hadn't a clue. 'I want to thank you and give you this', he said. 'You deserve it'. I accepted it politely. To be honest it meant nothing to me, and I just put it in my drawer back home. It's still there today, but I've kept it because it meant something to him."

vi) Class struggle

Our diagram is clear on the three-way consequences of labour's activities. The arrows represent in a simplified way what in social reality are complex social processes. Firstly there are the class practices which produce the means of subsistence for the population at large as well as the producers themselves. Secondly there are the developments of the producers themselves, both bodily as both personal and social means of production and so on, and subjectively in consciousness as well. Through consciousness and the use of existing cultural means, further working class culture is produced. Thirdly, there is also the resistance to social control coming from relationships entered into, which our theoretical position sees as always present in the face of such control over activities, however well meant. The outcome for relationships of this struggle between activities and control is the reproduction or transformation of those relationships. It is this third consequence of people's activities which yields the class conflict aspect of social reality. It is often assumed that class struggle is carried on intermittently by the producing class, but the evidence from social reality shows that in the broadest meaning of the term it is always present, often being waged most effectively by the owning and controlling classes. It is in the reproduction of the normality of everyday life that the ruling elites demonstrate their hegemony. Ironically the Thatcher government, in striving to return British society to its imagined nineteenth century normality by destroying the twentieth century "power of the trades unions", stimulated what Raphael Samuel called *radical conservatism*. The cultural underpinning of the government's activities was what we now know as `neo-liberalism`. At the time it was called `Thatcherism` or the New Right. It was promulgated in the last quarter of the twentieth century by Milton Friedman of Chicago University, and first practised on a "new society" in Chile after the murder of the democratically elected president Salvadore Allende by General Pinochet, Mrs Thatcher's friend. In opposition to this is an implicit ideology described by Samuel as follows,

> "The animating spirit of the 1984-5 strike – its `common sense` or implicit ideology – was that of *radical conservatism* . . . The miners were fighting against losing something, `defending what little we've got left,` as a miner put it in February 1985, speaking for a squad of men who had been reduced to picketing their own pit. Or, as a Maerdy woman put it to Barbara Bloomfield, `We just want to keep what we've got!`"

It is important to realise that ideologies are themselves objective cultural forms, even though they are held subjectively by people in historical activities, and that it is essential for historians/sociologists to have a cultural framework that gives them distance from the people they are studying. In this case by using a Marxist frame of reference and the concept of class struggle, we should not be understood as implying that our miners understood their situation in those terms. In the same way not all (or even any) of the miners saw themselves as radical conservatives.

Section 4. Empirical work: The miners' strike and the police

4a) Ideological struggle in the community

We will continue to approach our topic from the subjective element of social reality, looking at the activities and the thoughts, feelings and will of people involved in the relationships of the coal-pits, the NUM and the State. To situate the strike in what was then Northavon constituency, that is Yate & District, we will go through the local newspaper, the Thornbury Gazette, with the aim of locating reports of the strike and local people's public responses to it within some of the wider troubles and issues at the time. Availability of materials is not good, that is although most editions are still preserved, if somewhat scrappy, some important dates are missing. However, there is enough to form a systematic basis to begin our study. We will give quotations from the Gazette about the strike and related topics, placing them in the context of the reported concerns of the area. We will then outline the course of the strike as seen through the eyes of journalists and readers of the Gazette, giving direct quotes where possible. We will begin from the beginning of the year, three months before the strike started. The strike and the use of the police from the miners' point of view are graphically displayed in Mark Metcalf, Martin Jenkinson and Mark Harvey (2014) *Images of the Past: The Miners' Strike*, Barnsley, Pen & Sword Books. The text can also be used as a check on the view point of our account.

The main headlines of the Gazette dated 6th January 1984 were on one of the other strikes that rumbled on throughout the 1984: "**Aero workers defy strike call.** Eighty per cent of Rolls Royce APEX and ACTSS, whose members include white collar workers, did not obey their unions' call to strike on Bank Holiday over management running the Christmas and New Year holidays together. The strikers lost a day's pay". The TASS and ASTMS manual workers agreed with the merger as it gave them the feeling of more time away from work over the holiday. There is a measure of control class satisfaction in the tone of the report.

The Gazette of 15th January reported the activities of Andy Pott, Labour leader of Avon County Council, and John Channon, chairman of the Labour controlled Avon County Council. Jane Bradshaw and the Peace Group were also reported.

On January 20th Roger Berry reported on Labour's European vision. On January 27th and February 3rd Neil Kinnock's visit to Bristol is reported, and his support for local health unions against privatisation of the NHS. He is reported as attacking the Tories' re-orientation from "a Welfare State to a Warfare State." In the same edition, Dr. Fox is reported as trying to get a Government grant for 100% of the cost of a nuclear shelter, presumably to shield (some) people if the nuclear power station went wrong.

The Gazette of February 10th carries a press release of the AGM of Yate & Sodbury Labour Party in which the party chairman, Gordon Tily, said in his Annual Report, that 1983 had not been a good year for Yate Labour Party and that "We must prepare for a year of action in 1984". Mr.Tily reported the untimely death of Les Longley, the party's political officer. He said, "He was a good comrade and a good socialist who did his best to practice what he preached." The Labour Party had lost the 1983 general election, coming, for the first time, in third place to the Liberal/SDP Alliance. Mr Tily continued that Northavon CLP should concentrate its efforts on national and international issues, but that Yate branch should devote most of its efforts to local campaigns. The AGM elected Gordon Tily as Chair, Dorothy Struth as vice-chair, Ian Biddick as vice-chair, Bob Lomas as secretary, John Burge as treasurer, Roger Wilkins as membership secretary, Mike Chivers as press officer and Tony Williams as political officer.

Although the strike had begun in early March, there was nothing relevant in the Gazette until a month later. The general atmosphere in the Avon area into which the miners' strike was to descend can be seen in the April 6th edition. With headlines, **"Labour may lose traditional support"**, Tory MP Rob Haywood speaking at the AGM of Kingswood Conservative Association was reported as saying that Kingswood Labour Party was issuing more and more left-wing statements which would inevitably alienate their traditional supporters. He then switched his attack to Bristol Labour Party which, he said, was becoming ever more left-wing. An unrepresentative few in Bristol South had overthrown the moderate majority and the Labour MP, Michael Cox, was "now fighting for his political career at the whim of this unrepresentative few to the benefit of nobody". Mr. Hayward went on to criticise Marxism. He went on to say, "In St George East (Bristol) the Labour Party will be asking the local electorate to support a Marxist as their Council candidate. Marxism has never been a creed that has been acceptable to the people of this part of Bristol and if the policies that [the candidate] believes in are honestly argued during the election, they will reaffirm this through the ballot box at Bristol City Council elections" he said. To say the least, it seems odd that a Conservative should be so concerned that an opposition candidate should lose an election for whatever reason.

On April 20th 1984, the Gazette reported its first sighting of the now national miners' strike in the Northavon constituency.

<u>'Little Interest in Oldbury Pickets'</u>

'People living around Oldbury Power Station do not realise why it is being picketed by South Wales miners, or why thousands of miners are on strike throughout the country's coalfields, an Oldbury picket claimed this week.

The pickets from Blaenserchan [colliery in Pontypool, see map on page iv Hywel Francis (2009)], have been at the power station for four weeks and say that they will stay there for as long as their union is in conflict with the National Coal Board.

The eight men live in a cramped caravan which costs them £100 a week to rent. They work a shift system with twenty-four men doing a three-day rota: four sleeping and four outside the gates to keep a twenty-four hour picket line. But local people have shown little interest in them, and have neither welcomed them nor shown any hostility.

The men seemed surprised that the local population take little interest in the miners' strike. They say people do not seem interested in their points of view and the topic rarely surfaces in conversation when they go to Thornbury to shop or for a drink. "They have not been hostile and we have not been refused anything." They have been visited by trade unionists from Bristol with gifts of food, firewood and offers of help, but local people have shown little interest. "One of the butchers knocked down the price of some food for us, but most people don't seem bothered about us," said one of the men.

Their aim at Oldbury is to stop tankers passing the gates, and they claim that about fifty per cent of both union and non-union drivers have turned back.

Visitors to the picket line are surprised more support has not been given to the Oldbury pickets. The men show a certain independence and are not concerned at the low-key attitude towards their strike. "I don't want to ask anybody for something for nothing," one man said.`

Before we move on from this first report, it may be helpful to use it to illustrate our diagram above, and to place the report in the context of class analysis. The overall report begins with an apparent lack of understanding of the strike on the part of most of the local people, which the report does nothing to enlighten or explain. However, as a description of a fragment of social reality, the report covers all the elements. The second paragraph situates the men's activities in time, energy and space, and locates their position as one of class struggle. The third paragraph gives an account of their physical means, the caravan, and then moves on to the relations between the strikers and the locals, in this way developing the notion of an emerging social structure. The fourth paragraph describes the strikers' subjective response of surprise to their impressions from their interaction with the local population, whose lack of interest is quite different from that of people in their own communities. If we return to the evidence given by Fred Woodruff and Phyllis Taylor on page 20 above, then we can appreciate part of the reason for their surprise. The oral histories in Raphael Samuels (1986) show in clear detail the communities from which the miners had come. The fifth short paragraph continues the subjective element, although this time as the expression of their aims for future activities, rather than the impressions from their interactions with others. The final paragraph refers to the worker's value of independence, which is part of the cultural means shared by all traditional working class people, and especially by the mining communities. The concept of "attitudes" also refers to cultural means. It is important in all studies of labour history to understand that materialism does not focus simply on physical, or even biological means, but includes cultural (even "spiritual") means. Where producers' property is minimal, their ownership of cultural means may become that much more important. In this context it may be useful to note that throughout 1984 a constant topic in the Readers' Letters was "Virgin Birth", which I forbore to record here. The report also included a picture of eight men of the picket standing with a small placard reading "NUM Official Picket".

In the same edition there was a letter from a teacher referring to another strike that ran on parallel with the aero-engineers' and miners' strikes: It began:

`Teachers` 70 hour week`.

"Sir, Members of the public may be aware that school teachers are seeking a pay rise, and that members of one teachers` union have already taken strike action for an afternoon and refused to undertake any tasks which are not part of their contract e.g. lunchtime supervision, attendance at meetings and parent evenings. We perceive little support from the general public because many still believe the myth that we only work from nine until four o`clock and have long holidays. This myth is very far from the reality: there are teachers at the schools who work for seventy hours in a typical week . . ."

Northavon Constituency Labour Party held a *Solidarity with the Mineworkers* meeting for Labour Party and trade union members at the Holy Family School, Amberley Road, Patchway, Bristol, on Tuesday 24th April 1984 in the evening. Speakers included Des Dutfield, NUM executive committee member for the Rhondda and former vice-president of the South Wales NUM. The meeting was well attended and succeeded in its aim of building support for the mineworkers amongst members of the broad labour movement in Northavon and North Bristol.

The response to the miners` strike may not have been evident to the men on the picket line, but Readers` Letters of both support and often fierce opposition surfaced in the Gazette throughout 1984 and into 1985. In orientating research into expressions of attitude and opinion it is worth locating extremes at the beginning. One example comes from the veteran correspondent, Miss Olive Seller, supporter of Mrs Thatcher as the most adequate expression of conservatism, wrote on May 4th 1984:

Which way to Siberia Comrade?

Sir, Judging by Arthur Scargill's — and others of his radical ilk — past track record and vitriolic eloquence regarding the present Government's activities, this anti-establishment fanatic has but one goal in mind and that is the downfall of the current administration in London.

Unfortunately it appears he has no genuine concern, despite his protestation as champion of the workers, for the man-in-the-street, or he would respect the right to work and condemn picketing.

The garrulous miners' leader, secure in a comfortable and tolerant democracy, is obsessed with one motive, power over others.

One could find Mr. Scargill's beliefs amusing at a distance, but it seems that his particular brand of politics has found its way to our local Oldbury Power Station and such a close proximity to his "ruin the economy" hotline is extremely irritating.

What a pity this obviously pro-Russian "comrade" does not have the courage of his real conviction and emigrate to Siberia where the spartan climate would be more suited to his cloth-cap image.

Miss O. Seller, address supplied.

On May 18th there were two long letters supporting the miners in opposition to Miss Olive Sellers, of which I reprint the one from Roy Middleton, whose wife, Olive Middleton, was a Labour Party member and an active member of the Miners' Support Group.

Sir, I do not feel that even a letter from Miss O.Seller (Gazette May 4th) should be allowed to pass unremarked.

For her to label Arthur Scargill as `garrulous` is as ludicrous as Margaret Thatcher calling a political opponent `devious`, since we have been subject to Miss Seller's own brand of hyperbole for many years in the columns of this newspaper.

Were she to leave the comfort of her chair to talk to the peaceful and law-abiding pickets at local power stations or venture further afield into the mining areas of South Wales, she might arrive at a better understanding of the social and economic consequences of pit closures.

She would certainly find that the miners and their families are well able to make up their own minds and to argue their case in a direct and intelligible language, free from the pretentious wordiness and tortuous syntax she would have us believe are marks of intelligence.

It may well be true that we, in this `comfortable and tolerant democracy`, have much to be thankful for. If we do enjoy certain degrees of political freedom, these have been won for us by generations of ordinary working people, and are not there to be eroded by the most reactionary measures for half a century.

It is blinkered in the extreme to deny the many injustices and inequalities still existing within our society, and emotional rhetoric to suggest that those who are not totally satisfied with things as they are should `emigrate to Siberia`.

Roy Middleton, address supplied.

On May 25th the discussion in the Gazette shifted to concern with the policing of the miners` pickets. For a discussion of community policing versus the military-bureaucratic model see Mike Stephens and Saul Becker (1994) *Police Force, Police Service*, London, The Macmillan Press, especially pp. 222-227.

<u>Opposition to Avon Police`s Picket Duties.</u>

Avon and Somerset Police have been asked not to "hinder" miners` movements in Avon.

The Labour-controlled county council at last week`s annual meeting opposed the use of up to 190 local police on miners` picket lines.

Avon and Somerset chief constable Mr. Ron Broom was asked to give an assurance that police would not be used for "implied political purposes". Cllr Mike Thomas proposed the motion asking for the assurance and the move was supported by 33 votes to 27. Cllrs. supporting the motion agreed that freedom of movement in Britain was a long established principle. The council's newly elected chairman Cllr. Tom Turvey stated afterwards that the council had no say over operational police matters.

Members of Kingswood Labour Party Young Socialists have collected food items in Kings Chase shopping centre, Kingswood, and their latest effort was presented to South Wales miners last week.

In the following week's Gazette the editorial comment got serious about the constitutional implications of the council's request to the Avon and Somerset chief constable not to use the police for "implied political purposes".

"The Gazette June 1st 1984

The Policeman's Lot

County Hall politicians, never slow to seize an opening, appear to be embarking on a worrying course in criticising decisions to send local policemen to help maintain law and order on the picket lines. [However] it is right that the strength of the police forces left to maintain law and order in both Gloucestershire and Avon, while officers are drafted into the Midlands, should have been questioned.

Gloucestershire County councillors were told last week [that] a daily commitment of 127 men had been sent into Nottinghamshire and Warwick. In Avon 190 local police have been sent on picket duty. But while the levels of policing were rightly queried in both counties, Labour politicians in Avon went one dangerous step further and passed a resolution that the police should not be used for 'implied political purposes'. In a reference to mobile flying pickets, those supporting the motion agreed that freedom of movement n Britain was a long-established principle.

Although the motion was passed, it is likely to have a nil effect, for councillors who sit on county police committees have no say over how the police should operate. Nevertheless, it was a serious attempt to take the control of the police down a dangerous road on which police forces could end up being the servants of a country's political masters, whatever their shade of opinion."

The definition of the situation about the political use of the police is being seen here from two distinctive points of view. Thatcher's original use of the police against the miners is seen by Labour as political, but by the Gazette's editor as normal and non-political, whereas the Labour councillors` criticism of Thatcher is seen as "taking control of the police down a dangerous road. . .towards being servants of a country's political masters" i.e. towards Stalinist USSR.

"The police need to be above and apart from politics. There is a simple aim – to ensure that Britain's laws are upheld and law and order maintained. Let the politicians question police decisions in their counties. Let them air grievances and, where prejudices or poor policing methods are uncovered, let them criticise. But don't let them impose a particular political view on how their county's policemen and women should carry out their jobs. Any interference of this sort, putting local police forces under direct control of political parties, would be very dangerous indeed and a step toward the foundation of a police state."

Montesquieu's liberal 'separation of powers` principle which seats the rule of law in the separation of the three functions of the State, that are the legislature, the executive and the judiciary, is the editor's guide here. However valuable this was to the people who framed the constitution of the U.S.A., its fatal flaw is exposed in class analysis. All the evidence shows that the people who control the institutions of Parliament, the civil and armed services, the police and the legal system share the same class background, into which mobility is difficult and open only to strictly qualified individuals. The 1980s decision to use the neo-liberal ideology as the executive's guide to their long-term activity was made by these people. The logic of this ideology replaced production in manufacture with financialisation as the central activity of the British workforce; it replaced regulation of the distribution of goods and services with their marketisation; and it replaced the national relations of property with private ownership.

For empirical work and discussion of this, see Dexter Whitfield (2012) *In Place of Austerity,* Russell House, Nottingham, Spokesman [phone 0115 9708381]. Although it was not clear at the time, this was the ultimate reason for the miners' strike, the local government's decision to challenge the police authority's use of police personnel and the editor's difficulties with activities bridging the separation of powers.

The report of the County Council meeting claims that "Labour County Councillors have been slammed for a dangerous resolution to politicise the police". The report goes on: "Avon's Labour group supported a motion for assurance that the police would not hinder miners' movements in Avon and would not be used for 'implied political purposes'. . . But both Conservative councillors and Mr. Broome have lashed out at the resolution."

On the same page as the editorial of the Gazette, a letter from Miss O. Seller entitled *Violence on the Picket Line* answers the two pro-miners letters from Roy Middleton and R.S.Stopford, and ends,

"As for Scargill's pro-Russian affiliation being in doubt, his publicly avowed intention of 'overthrowing the Tories' certainly smacks more of the present repressive regime in the USSR, than a so-called democratic champion of the workers, whose vitriolic outbursts against authority are attempting to erode our present establishment.

Miss O. Seller (address supplied)"

By now local engagement in the discussion of the miners' strike seems to have reached a high point. Indeed Miss O. Seller's letter on June 8th indicates a subtle change of attitude towards policing.

<u>"In Praise of our Tolerant Police</u>

Sir, How right your leader (Gazette June 1st) was to highlight the danger of any particularly motivated body to attempt to handcuff the police, in their perfectly legal efforts to maintain law and order. Our police are the most tolerant, understanding and impartial force in this troubled world, and provocative and radical elements in the current picket activity outside pits have exploited this patient devotion to duty to the utmost. What with the appalling crime statistics, law-and-order in this once peaceful country is in mortal peril.
    Criticism of our law upholders is completely unjustified and denigrators should consider themselves lucky that our thin blue line does not (as in other countries) use tear gas, water cannons, and other repressive measures to quell mob rule. This **far-too-tolerant country** is a paradise for those who delight in baiting the police, and hurling not only missiles but also fabricated accusations of brutality.

While I hold no brief for the brutal regime abroad, a little more discipline would not come amiss, for the anarchy which is rearing its ugly head and disfiguring our democratic landscape is a blot which should be erased by a stronger application of authority.

Miss O. Seller etc"

On the 18th June 1984 at the Orgreave coking plant, near Rotherham, Yorkshire, about 8,000 miners gathered for a mass picket called by the NUM and their then President, Arthur Scargill. Accounts of what happened there given by the police and the miners differ considerably, but it has been the police account that has been accepted and absorbed into the popular memory. It is not that the miners' version has not received academic attention or that on the political left it has been forgotten, but that until 2008 popular capitalism as part of the neoliberal story had been established as common sense. It was these people whom Mrs Thatcher called "the enemy within", but it was not the miners who planted the bombs at the Conservative Party conference later that year which nearly killed her.The work of Greg Philo and the group calling themselves The Glasgow University Media Group give the original and best account of this in their book *Bad News*. This group was called by the leader of the then Conservative government's media enquiry, Lord Annan, "a shadowy guerrilla force on the fringe of broadcasting". Philo described their analysis as having "penetrated the surface appearance of neutrality and balance of the news media and found the partial and restricted reality."

In June the South West Regional Office sent to all its CLPs and women's organisations a photo of a mounted policeman with a raised baton bearing down on a member of Sheffield Women Against Pit Closures. The photograph was taken by John Harris at the Orgreave confrontation, and mirrored a famous painting of an incident in the 1905 Russian revolution. It was accompanied by a letter from the Regional Officer, Jean Corston (now Baroness Corston of St. George) reading,

"Dear colleague,

NUM DISPUTE

The enclosed photograph of a cutting from the front page of today's `Labour Weekly` graphically illustrates the political nature of this dispute and underlines the responsibility of each and every one of us to enable the miners to win. A very real fear in mining communities is that they will be forced back to work because of the effect of deprivation on their families. We must not let it happen. Continuing action is needed as follows."

There followed a list of actions recommended: donations, food, holidays, and children's clothing. This was followed by a list of miners` support centres in Cornwall, Devon, Somerset, Avon, Gloucestershire, Wiltshire and Dorset.

The then chairman of the Northavon CLP, George Lawrence, a retired docker from Newport, responded in his usual business-like way:

"I will provide a holiday for two striking miners` families: two wives and six children in total, at my caravan on the Gower coast. I will provide transport and some spending money. The date of the holiday is August 18th 1984 for a week.
 Any money which the Constituency Labour Party would be prepared to give towards this would be most helpful."

The CLP contributed £50 for the holiday. The offer was made as a personalised gift, accepted and greatly appreciated.

At the same meeting the then CLP secretary of the Northavon Constituency Labour Party was asked to write to Neil Kinnock conveying our support for the miners. He wrote:

"To the leader of the Labour Party June 4th '84

Dear Neil Kinnock,
                I have been asked by our G.C. to write to you about the miners' strike. We would like to congratulate you on your lead in urging all Labour Party members to give 50p a week to support the miners. This raised some smiles in some quarters, but in fact it has been surprising how many people in and around the Party, not normally active, have responded positively to this.

    The solidarity of the miners in defending their communities, their work and the future of their children has found an echo in many others in our decimated and fragmented society. This solidarity is the Labour movement's equivalent of the national `patriotism` created by the media in the Falklands War. It was this `patriotism` which was used by the Tories to win the 1983 election.

    I know that class struggle cannot be packaged by Saatchi and Saatchi as nationalism can, but we would urge that some lead be taken nationally to use this resource positively.

    Best wishes, fraternally,
        Colin Burgess, (secr.)"

So, locally Yate and District labour people were finding the wherewithal to support the miners in South Wales, to engage the Conservatives, and the Liberal/SDP Alliance when they surfaced, in the ideological struggle in the Gazette, and in Avon County Council. And nationally we were trying to agitate the powers-that-be to use the scarce resource of solidarity as effectively as the Tories used theirs. In the fullness of time we received the following reply from the Office of the Leader of the Opposition, though not from the Leader of the Labour Party, and thankfully not from "the Leader of Her Majesty's Loyal Opposition".

"Dear Mr. Burgess,   30 June 1984

Mr Kinnock has asked me to thank you for your letter of June 4 and to apologise for the delay in replying. This has been a very busy period. He hopes you understand.
He has asked me to reply on his behalf and to tell you that he very much hopes that the positive features which emerge in periods of collective action such as a national miners` strike can be used to strengthen the Labour Movement.

Yours sincerely etc"

These actions are as much part of Yate & District`s Heritage as descriptions of the technology used in local coal mines or the accumulated surplus value derived from the people of the area`s struggles to wrest scarce resources from Nature. We continue with the ideological struggle: first from a person who went on to become an LDP stalwart in Yate, then from a seasoned Conservative letter-writer, followed by a long letter from a Yate Labour Party activist.

"On Friday June 22nd

Not all of our policemen are wonderful

A very long letter from Chris Willmore LL.B. Lecturer in law, Bristol University, which opens

`Unlike many readers of the Gazette, I enjoy reading the regular contributions from Miss O. Seller of Thornbury, although I do not always agree with her. However, as a Barrister and University lecturer in law I feel compelled to write to correct some of the comments she makes.`"

I do not wish to lay out in this place the content of the ideological struggle between the Liberal-democrats and the Conservatives, merely to note that it was taking place, therefore I shall not go into Ms Willmore's reasoning here. The following week saw the veteran Tory M.J. Radnege's contribution:

"Weird View of the Police

Sir, How I deplore the letter headed "Not All Our Policemen are Wonderful", written by a Liberal. It is disgusting to suggest that we should educate our children etc."

By now the discussion has widened to focus on the periphery of the main concern. I would like to bring it back to the miners' strike with another long letter, this time from Mike Chivers, a long time member of the Labour Party, whose concerns centre on labour history. His letter is dated July 6th 1984.

"Sir, I would like to comment on Chris Willmore's letter (Gazette 22 June) concerned with the police. The letter deals only with a narrow viewpoint of the police and the people who are employed as policemen. The problem to which the letter should have been addressed is the relationship between the legal system and the community. The legal system is a mirror of the values which the society has of justice and of freedom, and is supposed to be above bias and equal to all people.

The solution is that there should be a truly accountable police force committed to the maintenance of law and order on the basis of real respect for individual liberty of all sections of the community. This can be achieved if the tradition of a citizen police force is maintained. The separation of the police force from the rest of the community, and the growing distrust which some sections of the community have of the police is disturbing.

The present conflicts, for example the miners' dispute and the Greenham Common peace protest show that the police are supporting only one interest. This means that certain interests have a power which other people do not.

The differences within an area should be the basis for the creation of a community police council. The councils would provide an opportunity for open discussion between the police and the community as to the quality and manner of police provision. The membership of these councils would be drawn from local councillors and a wide range of community groups.

The result of a greater accountability is that the police will win the confidence of the whole community. The police must develop a close and continuous relationship with the community and to draw on its resources to help to control crime as well as giving people a real say in the way society is policed.

Mike Chivers, address supplied."

Mr. Chivers` belief that the police should be equally available to all sections of the community is what is required in a socialist society. The notion that it can be achieved in a capitalist society is an example of the liberal-democratic ideology that masks the relations between the State, monopoly capitalism and globalisation. The following week June 13th carried a letter from H.R.Pike, Staple Hill police station, Bristol in which he wrote that he had read with interest Mr. Mike Chivers` letter on the question of the police and the public. He said that he wished to point out that police authority liaison committee meetings are open to all interested parties. On a present day note, it will be interesting to observe the effects that the newly elected Commissioners on Police and Crime have in practice on crime and the perception of crime. In the same week a further notice of the miners` dispute appeared, probably submitted by Mr. Chivers as Northavon`s press officer.

"Miners put their case

Three miners from the picket at Oldbury power station, Thornbury, sat in on last week`s meeting of the Severndale [?] Labour Party. The three pointed out that if the coal industry shrank so would British industry generally. Since 1981 10,000 jobs had been lost in the Bristol area. In the next four years it could be 20,000. They said that coal mined in Great Britain was cheaper than anywhere else in the world. Other countries subsidised their coal, Britain didn't."

It may have been a meeting of the Thornbury and Severnvale Branch Labour Party to which this notice referred, as that branch met on Wednesday 6th June, the week before the notice was published. If so the response would have been interesting as George Lawrence, Olive Middleton and Colin Burgess definitely supported the miners, whereas other members had closer links with the atomic energy industry.

On 20th July the report from Avon and Somerset's chief constable was headlined, "Picket duty bill tops £1 million". The chief constable revealed that no payment had been received to date for the local police sent for picket duty, referred to as "mutual aid". The costs included an overtime bill of £15,000, and costs for hiring and replacing vehicles, mileage and additional administration.

Throughout July and August there are letters and reports on current issues such as Labour's call for a general hospital for Yate, and a meeting with leading county councillors called by Yate Labour Party to discuss the Government's plans to expand Yate. However, reports of concern about the miners' strike were replaced by reports on developments in the aero industry's local dispute. On August 3rd both sides were reported to be "firm" in the lockout. The strikers had responded by blockading Filton aeroplant.

On August 24th the editorial was entitled "Bristol Fashion" and read as follows:

"Industrial action – some would prefer it termed inaction – has taken a worrying new turn. Thousands if not millions of pounds of taxpayers' money is being spent on policing the miners' strike in an attempt to ensure some semblance of law and order generally and protection for those who wish to work in particular.

At Filton last week there was a much more low-key dispute. Thankfully on this occasion all ended peacefully with smiling constables carefully hoisting away pickets who had been blockading the Bristol British Aerospace works . . .The actions are worrying on two principle counts:

1.	There is the time and cost of employing local policemen to keep an eye on these disputes, and then having to use them to enforce injunctions imposed by the courts. This is public time and money regardless of the justification of what is in effect a private dispute between employer and employee;

2.	There is the long-term effect of turning the public's gaze on such irresponsible actions. The National Coal Board has said that the miners' dispute will lose future orders. At B.Ae. the local MP, John Cope, has warned that it is important for the Filton plant not to get a bad image."

A report in the body of the newspaper read, "Blockade gives way to pickets at B.Ae."

4 b) Discussion of Gazette readers' letters

The letters to the Gazette reveal deep divisions of attitude and opinion on the class struggle, which are not normally on display. It is possible that most of the letter-writers would not consider themselves as taking part in an ideological struggle at all. This phrase comes from the sociological perspective we have used to analyse the letters, to locate them into categories of "for and against" rather than as the expression of deeply held opinions, from which the opinions flow. The problem for most people unused to this perspective is that for its use it requires a clear statement of its orientation to the object being viewed. The orientation includes a statement of both theory and method used, that is, the methodology for the analysis. For example most history is studied and written from the viewpoint of the "liberal middle-class" perspective of the historian. The refined perspectives based on the the work of Max Weber, Emile Durkheim or Karl Marx, and the traditions of research following those perspectives are not normally used knowingly. However, the gains in clarity made from their use is worth the effort made in coming to understand them.

Section 5. Class struggle: the miners' strike in historical materialist perspective

For work done on this section see, for example, Mark Metcalf et al (2014) *Images of the Past: the Miners' Strike*, Barnsley, Pen & Sword Books Ltd. especially chapters 1 and 2.

5 a) The ruling class and the miners

We have so far described the national miners' strike in the context of the local Constituency Labour Party, and the industrial disputes. However, because of the historical importance of the actions of the National Miners' Union, we now wish to raise the level of both the description of the activities of the people involved, and the analysis of the background to the strike. The theoretical basis of the analysis is provided by Marxist thought, and the focus on the people involved shifts to the ruling class Government of the day. The historical background is the onset of the second major slump of the twentieth century, which following a personalised Keynesian solution, allowed credit to be increasingly available to provide homes for people who were increasingly unable to repay the loans. The other liberal democratic solution was to complete the destruction of working class power by destroying the trades union. Given the destruction of working class institutional power, in situations of conflict and resistance, the emergence of violence becomes at least most probable.

Because of the wide-spread use of the liberal democratic ideology today, it is necessary to operationalise the concept of "the ruling class" for observation and empirical work. A useful contemporary statement comes from Robert Griffiths (General Secretary of the

Communist Party of Britain) `The ruling class is alive and well` in *The Morning Star* August 11th 2009.

"Who comprises the British ruling class?

The controlling shareholders – British residents and tax exiles – of the handful of giant companies which together monopolise the main sectors of finance, commerce and the mass media, who provide the basis of its economic power. Many of these shareholders are also company directors whose multiple directorships and investments knit the capitalist monopolies into a single matrix, the links multiplied and reinforced by bank loans.

These are among the 5 percent of Britain`s adult population, who according to the Inland Revenue, own more than half (58%) of Britain`s wealth. The poorer half of the population own just 1 percent, down from 6 percent on the eve of New Labour`s election triumph in 1997. The poorest three-quarters (which would approximate to the working class) own 15 percent.

The permanent staff at the top of the different sections of the state apparatus, including the Civil Service, the judiciary, the armed forces and the police and intelligence services constitute the executive arm of the ruling class. The BBC, the state church and the education system reflect and reinforce ruling class ideas, although the processes by which this happens are more subtle, complex and contested than should be imagined – and all the more effective as a result.

The myriad ways in which the economic power of the monopolies fuses with the political power of the state gives rise to the concept of `state monopoly capitalism` to explain the economic and political system as it exists today."

The conflict of values and interests between the ruling class and the working class today are masked by the expansion of the technological and social control class mediating the polarising classes, and the globalisation of monopoly capital, both industrial and financial. The ideological mix veiling the conflict in Britain contains feudal elements (the Royal personages, properties and Church and State duties), capitalist elements (personal wealth and power, and the value for "freedom" and competition), and democratic elements (liberal-democratic ideology). For a useful sociological discussion, see John Scott (1991) *Who Rules Britain?* Cambridge, Polity Press.

5 b) Contemporary class struggle

Contemporary class struggle becomes visible again from 1975 onwards, and is marked by the renewal of the ruling class attempts to protect the owners` declining profits as the long wave boom came to an end. In the period of Parliamentary opposition from 1974 they began seriously to organise themselves to re-take the long-term gains of national living standards that had been made through Labour's partial victories in developing the "welfare" state.

We have referred above to the miners` strike of 1984-5 as an event similar to our postal workers` strike of 2009 in that both were not merely to do with forms of control and resistance, although that was part of the situation. Both were struggles over the transformation and reproduction of society, that is, the relationships of social reality, and both were part of the same ongoing struggle. The Conservative Party's strategy which co-ordinates their activities is written in the Ridley Plan, developed under Nicholas Ridley's chairmanship of the Economic Reconstruction Group in 1977. This meeting marks the hard-edged beginning of the embedment of neo-liberal ideology in Britain, which was more or less softly completed by Mr Blair from 1997. On the effects of the "Ridley Plan" see Owen Jones (2012) chapter two, especially pages 54-60.

The opposition of the trades unions to Edward Heath's government, from the T.U.C's refusal to register as Friendly Societies to the miners' strike of 1974, brought the government down. In the wake of this defeat, Sir Keith Joseph commissioned Nicholas Ridley as Under-Secretary of State for the Department of Trade and Industry (DTI) to report on future Conservative Party industrial policy. The final report was prepared by the Conservative Research Department and discussed by the Economic Reconstruction Group of the Nationalised Industry Policy Group on Friday 8th July 1977 in the Westminster Hall Interview Rooms at the House of Commons. The chair of the meeting was Nicholas Ridley. This policy document re-oriented British government away from the social functions of the State into the repressive functions supporting capitalism. The Ridley Report is comparable with the CDP's Report, being aimed at the regeneration of British society, but having a much broader remit and effects. The Ridley Report was based on the Chicago School economics of Milton Friedman, as the note on "denationalisation" on page 18. Point 1a) makes clear, "We could give one share to each person whose name is on the Electoral Roll (an idea advocated by Friedman)." Judging by events that have happened since, all governments have used this document as a blue-print for their activities. On the other hand, the CDP Report based on a Marxist historical understanding seems to have been quietly dropped. It is interesting that the CDP Report on a suburb of Newcastle, entitled *The Making of a Ruling Class,* shows how Nicholas Ridley's family and kinship wealth originated in the coal-mining industry before taking flight into the financial sphere. On Milton Friedman, Friedrich Von Hayek, Enoch Powell, Nicholas Ridley, Keith Joseph, Alfred Sherman and Norman Tebbit, see the introduction to John Ranelagh (1991) *Thatcher's People* and Chapter One for their interaction with Thatcher herself. The focus on people in this book serves to supplement the institutional and structural focus of the rest of the book. The relations between Thatcher and the ruling class has been nicely put by Owen Jones (2014) p.53 – 54,

"In the first decades after World War II, the Tories had been dominated by the paternalistic 'One Nation' tradition – to which Macmillan subscribed – founded by the nineteenth-century. It was this group who – much to the disdain of the outriders – had accepted the post-war consensus, and who had reservations or fears about the new neo-liberal order. Under Thatcherism, they became marginalised to the point of non-existence."

It is difficult to find a more ready example of the activities of the ruling class than those around Ridley at this time. He was a member of the National Association for Freedom (NAFF), which was "a network of senior military and intelligence figures, senior industrialists and cabinet ministers, its members included [the young] Winston Churchill, Jill Knight, David Mitchell, Rhodes Boyson, and Nicholas Ridley". The NAFF had been set up Brian Crozier, a journalist who worked for both British intelligence and the CIA, and Norris McWhirter, Lord De L'Isle, Michael Ivens of Aims of Industry, [the young] Winston Churchill MP, merchant banker John Gouriet and Robert Moss [Mrs Thatcher's speech-writer] [source: BAP Primer, Transatlantic Elite – British American Project for the successor generation]. These constitute what Robert Griffiths called the "executive arm of the ruling class" see page 134. Brian Crozier also ran the Institute for the Study of Conflict (ISC) a right-wing propaganda group set up by British and American intelligence people. In 1976 Crozier also set up a committee called Shield, to advise Mrs Thatcher and three other members of her shadow cabinet, Lord Carrington, Sir Keith Joseph, and William Whitelaw, who would later become Lord Whitelaw. John Ranelagh, who was at the Conservative Research Department between 1975 and 1979, and so probably involved in the writing of the Ridley Report, describes the complexity of the Tory, Unionist and Conservative groupings vying for control of the Conservative Party at the time. Then, separate from these groups, but including all of them, there were three further groups competing for control of the Party: the traditional ruling group, the Thatcherite "lower middle class in politics" group, and a third "Conservative Party" group, still anti Edward Heath but mediating between the first two groups. See John Ranelagh (1992) *Thatcher's People*, London, Fontana, chapter two.

The supposedly secret Ridley Report was leaked in *The Economist* in 1978. Given the contents it appears to have been used by both neo-liberals and their opposition, both the controllers and their resistance. Part 1 of the Report, *Running Nationalised Industries*, starts with a section on "Motivation". Discipline in the public sector is weaker than in the private sector, there being no possibility of bankruptcy and no hope of rewards from higher dividends. Ridley's solution is to bring the sticks and carrots from the private sector into the public sector. The Report continues with a discussion of how this can be done.

One of the problems with Robert Griffiths' identification of our contemporary social reality is that the term State Monopoly Capitalism can be reduced to where to insert a hyphen. For Griffiths it is State Monopoly-Capitalism, for Ridley it is State-monopoly capitalism. For Griffiths it is the economic power of the privately owned capitalist monopolies like British Petroleum or Tesco's and the associated political power of the capitalist State. For Ridley the problem is the lack of market discipline over the publicly owned state monopolies like the nationalised industries as they were in the 1970s or the NHS today. Even the old Liberal John Stuart Mill's notion of "natural monopolies" like the railways should not be exempt from competition and the market's carrots and sticks. Ridley's equivalent `stick` for the public monopolies would be neither coercion, nor moral commitment, but `remuneration`. The other monopoly that his people were eager to rid themselves of was the "trade union monopoly of labour". This idea comes directly out of the free enterprise school of economics. However, Ridley believed that making strikes illegal would cause the maximum political "aggro" without worthwhile results, and he expressly rejected the idea of a strike-breaking corps of trained volunteers standing by to run the mines, the trains or the power stations. This view seems to support John Saville's third factor, the recognition by the property owners of the price that has to be paid for political security. This makes the events of Orgreave Colliery all the more interesting. Remunerative control is the market discipline that he favours. His view is that governments should insist that nationalised industries produce a return on the capital invested that is in line with private investment. In a similar way the state should deprive strikers of welfare benefits. This is the way that the State would control labour and "socialism" through the market.

5 c) Privatisation and the boundary between state monopoly-capitalism and liberal-democratic ideology

However the purpose of a Conservative government is not to run the nationalised industries, but to rid the nation of such monopolies. As Enoch Powell said in the early 1960s, "The nationalised industries are a foreign body in the British economy, and a dagger pointing at the heart of the Conservative Party. They must be removed." The long term policy aim, which runs throughout the Ridley Report, is summed up in one word, "Fragmentation". The political objective, they say, must be to fragment the public sector of industry into a number of independent units, which could eventually be denationalised, or "privatised", as we would say today in line with the ideology of individualism. The fragmentation of working class consciousness and solidarity is a possibly unintended consequence of this policy. Dexter Whitfield (1983) *Making it Public: Evidence and action against privatisation*, London, Pluto Press examined the creation of myths and propaganda that followed the circulation of the Ridley Report. He takes statements by people and organisations of the political right, which state myths about privatisation and, from the view-point of labour, contrasts them with facts about the situations referred to. These are:

"Myth one: privatisation creates a company-owning democracy
Myth two: privatisation increases our freedom
Myth three: privatisation eliminates waste
Myth four: privatisation will revive the economy
Myth five: privatisation saves money."

Without reiterating Whitfield's refutation of the myths, I just wish to quote the first myth as relevant to the discussion of the meeting between Keith Joseph, Mrs. Thatcher, Nicholas Ridley and the Nationalised Industry Policy Group of the Conservative Party's Economic Reconstruction Group held on 8th July 1977.

"Myth 1: privatisation creates a company-owning democracy

Example of the propagation of the myth by Nicholas Ridley, from *The Public Sector for the Public* [this is the title of the Economic Progress Report, Treasury, May 1982].

> 'The introduction of competition must whenever possible be linked to a transfer of ownership to private citizens and away from the state. Real public ownership – that is ownership by people – must be and is our ultimate goal'. (Nicholas Ridley, Financial Secretary to the Treasury, 12th February 1982)

This statement illustrates the Tory tactic of convincing people that privatisation is a means of spreading wealth and ownership, that more and more people are buying shares and benefitting from the capitalist system. The reality is completely different. This does not deter the Tories."

Whitfield goes on to demonstrate the way that shares in British Aerospace, Cable and Wireless, Amersham International, Britoil and Associated British Ports, rose in price and that over time they became more and more concentrated in the financial institutions like banks, pension funds, insurance companies and investment trusts. A test of the hypothesis that there is a systemic pressure in capitalism to the concentration and centralisation of capital can be checked by tracing the movement of Royal Mail shares in 2013. A test of a hypothesis from an alternative perspective can be made by checking the notion that worker-owners buying out or being given shares in privatised industries will lead to wider ownership. Whitfield writes,

> "Theoretically, management or worker buy-outs will also lead to a spread in ownership. Collectively, however, workers will only have a tiny percentage share and no real control of the firm through ownership. What they will have, of course, is the illusion of ownership and the illusion of a vested interest in the firm's profitability. This is really what the Tories are after. They hope to create a new breed of worker-capitalists, more concerned with increasing annual dividends by cutting production costs than with the protection of their working conditions." Pp 28-31

The value of Whitfield's analysis here is that his five myths and the effects of the "illusions" mark the boundaries between state monopoly-capitalism and liberal-democratic ideology, and the lifting of a corner of the mystical veil, revealing the ruling class. The ideology has two sides: the neo-liberal aspect and the mass democratic (or even populist) aspect – these aspects cast the shadows on the walls of Plato's cave. An understanding of this is the beginning of political wisdom.

Before leaving the Ridley Report, it is important to discuss briefly the influence of Brian Crozier on British politics. A group calling itself wakeupmag.co.uk published a document entitled *The Psyops War: British Intelligence and the Covert Propaganda Front and the CIA's Interference in British Politics* (No date but after 1997). The document is available on:

http://www.american-buddha.com/cia.psyops.htm

On the origins of British post-war psyops, they write,

> "In 1948, a secret political/psychological warfare department known as the Information Research Department (IRD), was set up within the Foreign Office, with the aim of embarking on a "propaganda offensive" against the left. To conceal the operation's existence from the public, its funding was obtained from Parliament on "the secret vote".

The IRD had two main purposes. It created "grey" propaganda for overseas' consumption, which was directed against "Communism", a catch-all label that included anything remotely left-wing or anti-imperialist. The primary targets were Western Europe and South East Asia, followed by India, Pakistan and the Middle East. (The Soviet Union was left largely to American intelligence). The IRD's second area of action was the moulding of domestic opinion in Britain. It used anti-Communist material created with government funds to aid right-wing social democrats within the Labour Party and the trade union movement. Christopher Mayhew, the Foreign Office minister who set up the IRD, later reported to his boss, Ernest Bevin, that he had made arrangements with Herbert Tracey, public secretary of the Trades Union Congress, "for the dissemination inside the Labour movement at home of anti-Communist propaganda which we are producing for overseas consumption".

The CIA and its ideological struggle against Communism, which in Britain focused particularly on the magazine *Encounter*, is well documented by Francis Stonor Saunders (1999) *Who Paid The Piper*, London, Granta Books. This is supported by Lynn Walsh and Richard Fletcher (1982) *CIA infiltration of the Labour Movement*, London, Militant. Further work on anti-State provision of services is available from the Institute of Economic Affairs, the right-wing research and educational charity, for example, Arthur Seldon (1996) IEA Readings

45, *Re-privatising Welfare: After the Lost Century*, London, IEA. Also see chapters two and three, pages 7 to 27 of Mark Metcalf, Martin Jenkinson and Mark Harvey (2014)

Spying activities have not been confined to historical foreign intervention in British politics. The activities of the Metropolitan Police Special Demonstration Squad The Morning Star Saturday/Sunday March 14/15th 2015 reports, " Peter Francis, a former agent with the Metropolitan Police Special Demonstration Squad, told a meeting in Parliament late on Thursday night [12th March 2015] that he had spied on public sector workers – firefighters, teachers, and postmen – as part of his undercover duties. . . In a statement read out by Labour MP John McDonnell at the launch of the new book, *Blacklisted*, Mr. Francis said he wished to "unreservedly apologise to all the union members I personally spied upon and reported back on whilst deployed undercover in the SDS."

Section 6. Conclusions

We have attempted to show in this study how the miners` strike of 1984/5 is situated in present-day society, and the contemporary sociology and history of Britain. This requires the controlled use of the tsunami of information and theoretical work available through the electronic media. We move from the local CLP`s response to the government`s use of mounted police to control the miners` resistance to the closure of the coal mines to the geo-political anti-communism of United States` foreign policy. As part of the resistance to the elimination of Britain`s industrial base, and the State`s development of London as a global financial hub, the miners stood firm for over a year against Capital`s war on Labour. Their defeat allowed the extension of Capital`s destructive power to open the National Health Service to global capital. The widely proclaimed "Tory War on the Poor" flooded in on the wake of that defeat. The miners` defence of our national life should become part of the "One

Nation Labour" heritage before the popular memory is erased by the deliberate ephemera of the mass media.

We have also consciously used this little study to guide a small group of amateur historians in the use of methods of study helpful for people concerned with "history and sociology from below". This is not a text-book on how to write polemical leaflets or articles, which is best left to members of established socialist groups like the Socialist Workers Party, but as an attempt to re- open Marxian perspectives in the Labour Party. Edward Palmer Thompson is a useful introduction to the New Left tradition of writing "History from below", see for example Cal Winslow (2014) and the older book by R.S. Neale (1985) especially chapter 7, Class and Urban History, and the Historian`s Task.

Reading List

Christopher J. Arthur (2002) *The New Dialectic and Marx`s Capital* Leiden, Brill
Seumas Milne (2004) *The Enemy Within: the secret war against the miners,* London, Verso: third edition.

Benwell Community Project (1979) *Final Report,* Series no. 6 *The Making of a Ruling Class*, Newcastle upon Tyne, Benwell Community Project
Huw Beynon (1985) ed. *Digging Deeper: Issues in the miners` strike.* London, Verso
Catherine Paton Black (2012) *At the Coal Face: my life as a miners` wife*, London, Headline Publishing Group
Lorna Brooks & David Hardills (2008) *Anti-slavery in South Gloucestershire* Yate & District Heritage Centre

E.H. Carr (2001) 2nd edn. *What is History?* Houndmills, Palgrave

Velichko Dobrianov `The Marxist Sociological Paradigm`, in A.G. Zdravomysolov ed. (1986) *Developments in Marxist Sociological*

Theory, modern social problems and theory, London, Sage Publications Inc.

Steve Grudgings et al (2009) *Frog Lane Colliery – sixty years on*, Yate, South Glos Mines Research Group (SGMRG) and the Yate & District Heritage Centre
Steve Grudgings et al (2008) *Kingswood Coal*, Yate, SGMRG and the Yate & District Heritage Centre

Eric Hobsbawm (1969) *Industry and Empire*, London, Penguin Books

Owen Jones (2012) *Chavs: the demonization of the working class*, London, Verso

Owen Jones (2014) *The Establishment, and how they got away with it*, London, Allen Lane

Mark Metcalf et al (2014) *Images of the Past: The Miners' Strike*, Barnsley, Pen & Sword Books Ltd.

R.S.Neale (1985) *Writing Marxist History: British Society, Economy & Culture since 1700*, Oxford, Basil Blackwell Ltd

Bertell Ollman (1993) *Dialectical Investigations*, London, Routledge

Raphael Samuel (1986) *The Enemy Within: pit villages and the miners' strike of 1984-5*, London, Routledge & Kegan Paul

Goran Therborn (2012) *Class in the Twenty-first Century*, London, New Left Review 78 Nov/Dec 2012
Goran Therborn (2014) *New Masses?* London, New Left Review 85 Jan/Feb 2014

Cal Winslow (2014) *E.P.Thompson and the making of the New Left* New York, Monthly Review Press

A.G. Zdravomysolov ed. (1986) *Developments in Marxist Sociological Theory, modern social problems and theory,* London, Sage Publications Inc.

Newspapers

Editions of Thornbury Gazette for 1984 and 1985 stored in Thornbury Library.
Editions of The Morning Star, from newsagents.

Index

A

AGM of Yate and Sodbury Labour Party 1983:
page 27
AGM of Kingswood Conservative Party1983:
page 28
Salvadore Allende:
page 25
Austerity
page 36
Avon County Council: Andy Potts and John Chanon:
page 27
Avon and Somerset Police:
page 33

B

Baptist Mills:
page 21
Roger Berry MP:
page 27
Catherine Paton Black:
page 2
Jane Bradshaw:
page 27
Brass:
pages 10, 16, 21
Bristol:
pages 22, 28, 31,
British Aerospace:
page 44
Bristol and the Slave Trade:
pages 4, 7-8, 10-14

Colin Burgess:
pages 39-40

C

Capitalism:
pages 5, 11, 12
Central Intelligence Agency (CIA):
page 54
Chicago University:
page 25
Chile:
page 25
Mike Chivers:
pages 41-43
Class:
pages 3-9
Class Structure:
pages 6-8 11-14
Class struggle:
pages ix, 2, 24-26, 48-51
Class Interests:
pages 6-8 14-17
Class Practices:
pages 6, 8, 17-19
Class Community:
pages 20-22
Class Consciousness, development of:
pages 20-24
Coalpit Heath:
pages 12-13, 16, 20
Edward Colston:
page 11
Communist Party; communism and anti-communism:
pages 24, 46, 54

Joseph Conrad:
page 16
Conservative Party/Association/Government:
pages 38, 48-50, 52
Controllers:
pages 13-14
Jean Corston, secretary, South West Regional Office:
pages 38-39
Handel Cossham:
pages 12-14, 21
BrianCrozier:
pages 49, 54

D

Abraham Darby:
pages 16, 21
Jeremy Delle:r:
.page 2
Fred Drew:
pages 15, 17, 21
Emile Durkheim and the concept of ` function`:
page 45
Des Dutfield:
page 31

E

Economic Reconstruction Group:
page 48
Empire:
pages 10-11
The Enemy Within:
pages 1, 38

F

Feudalism:
pages 11, 12, 48
Fragmentation:
pages 40, 50-52
Milton Friedman:
page 25
Frog Lane:
pages 20-22
Social Functions
pages 4, 10, 14, 21

G

The Gazette:
pages 2-3, 9, 26-45
Glasgow University Media Unit:
page 38
Greenham Common:
page 42
Robert Griffiths:
pages 46-47
Guinea Goods:
page 10

H

John Harris:
page 38
Edward Heath MP:
page 48
History Workshop:
pages 1-2

I

Independence:
page 30
Institute of Economic Affairs (IEA):
page 55

J

Owen Jones:
pages 48-49
Keith Joseph MP:
pages 48, 50

K

Kingswood coal mines:
pages 13, 17
Neil Kinnock MP:
pages 39-40
Kondratiev long-wave economic activity
page ix

L

Labour MPs, Early Day Motion (EDM):
page 1
Labour Party:
pages 3, 20, 23, 27-28, 31-34, 39-45, 55-56
Labour Party Young Socialists:
page 34
Ian Lavery MP:
page 1
George Lawrence, chairman of Northavon CLP:
pages 39, 43

Leopold II, King of the Belgians:
page 16
Liberal-democratic ideology
page viii

M

Karl Marx and the concept of `social reality`:
pages 19, 45
Marxism:
pages 25, 28, 45-46, 49
Maerdy Women`s Support Group:
page 3
Mapping social reality:
pages 5-6
Meaning of the strike:
pages 21-25, 28-30
Meaning of work:
pages 17-25
Olive Middleton::
pages 32-33, 43
RoyMiddleton:
pages 32-33
Miners` Strike:
pages 1-2, 5, 7-9, 18, 25-31, 35-45, 48-49,
Montesquieu:
page 35
Mosaic
page 4

N

National Association for Freedom (NAFF):
pages 49-50
National Coal Board:
page 45

National Union of Miners:
page 46
Nationalised Industry Policy Group:
pages 49, 52
National Health Service:
page 56
Neo-liberalism:
page 25
New Labour:
pages 7, 46
Northavon CLP:
pages 31, 39

O

Oldbury pickets:
page 28-29, 32, 43
Orgreave coking plant: mass picket:
page 2, 37, 38
Owners:
pages 13, 18, 22

P

Peace Group:
page 26
Picket line:
pages 28-29, 31, 33-34, 36
General Pinochet:
page 25
Plato:
page 54
Police picket duties:
page 33
Postal workers:
page 48

popular memory:
pages 1-2
post-modernism
page 5
Enoch Powell:
pages 51-52
privatisation:
pages 48-55
producers:
pages 16-19

R

Radical Conservatism:
page 25
Red Star:
page 24
Relationships
pages 11-14, 24
Resistance:
pages 5, 18, 24, 46, 48, 56
Nicholas Ridley MP; Ridley Report:
pages 48-54
Ruling Class:
pages 46-51

S

Raphael Samuel:
pages 1-2, 7- 8, 25
SARM:
pages 5-7
Arthur Scargill:
pages 31-33, 36-37
Miss Olive Sellers:
pages 31-37

Sheffield Women Against Pit Closures:
page 38
Slave trade:
pages 5, 10-11, 16, 21-22
St. George:
pages 13, 28, 38
State monopoly-capitalism:
pages 49-51

T

Phyllis Taylor:
pages 20-21
Teachers Strike:
pages 30-31
Mrs Thatcher MP:
pages 24-25, 38, 48-52
Gordon Tiley:
page 27

U

Upward social mobility:
pages 12-14

V

Value (necessary and surplus):
pages 15-16
Violence on the Picket Line:
page 36; for additional images of violence on the picket lines see Sean Matgama (2014) pages 9, 26, 36, below and Mark Metcalf et al (2014) below.
Virgin Birth:
page 30

W

Max Weber and the concept of `meaning`:
page 45
Westerleigh:
 pages 12-16
DexterWhitfield:
pages 35, 51-53
Winterbourne:
page 20
Women`s Support Group:
pages 3, 38
FredWoodruff:
page 20, 22
Working Class:
 pages 3-5, 10-26

Y

Yate & District Heritage Centre:
 pages 3-4, 7
Yate & Sodbury Labour Party:
page 27
Young Socialists
page 34

<u>Space for Notes</u>